Paljon Onnea
Tealle
Ilonan-päivänä
1996 –
Äiti

NATURE LIBRARY

*

BONSAI

The author wishes to specially thank Dr Leila Dhanda whose creations kindled her interest in the art of bonsai. As President Emeritus of the Indian Bonsai Association Dr Dhanda has been a constant source of encouragement and advice. To her and her book, *Bonsai Culture*, the author owes the inspiration and guidance to write this book.

ISBN: 1-85605-296-6

Published by **Blitz Editions**
an imprint of
Bookmart Limited
Registered Number 2372865
Trading as Bookmart Limited
Desford Road
Enderby, Leicester, LE9 5AD

Project Coordinator: Padmini Mehta
Text Editor: Bela Butalia
Photographs: Dheeraj Paul
Design: Sarita Verma Mathur
Typesetting: Monika Gupta

Printed and bound by
Star Standard Industries Pte. Ltd., Singapore

NATURE LIBRARY

BONSAI

Kiran Misra

Blitz Editions

FOREWORD

It is with great pleasure that I recommend this little book to the ever-growing bonsai public. A beginner in this art will find it a boon for his or her bonsai career. This art is gathering deserved popularity at a very rapid rate. Knowledge of natural history is essential for making a bonsai and in understanding and visualising the way a tree grows.

Though small in size, this is a concise and easy to read and understand book. The drawings and photographs will also be of great help in initiating a bonsai 'hopeful' in this art. It may not be known that this art originated in China whence it spread to Japan. During the Second World War many American soldiers were stationed in Japan and thus the art was spread by them to the Western countries. It is only 40 years since a few hardy souls began to develop the first bonsais in India but partly due to increased urbanisation and the consequent lack of garden space, the love for gardening has had to be represented by pot culture in verandahs, terraces and roofs. Therefore bonsai culture, which is a highly developed form of pot culture, has reaped the benefit of these situations.

With these few words let me wish the book and of course the author the best of luck, and may the bonsai art flourish more and more.

DR LEILA DHANDA

ACKNOWLEDGEMENTS

The author would like to acknowledge the following sources which she consulted extensively while preparing her book:

Christian Pessey, *Bonsai. A Step by Step Guide*. London, 1994.
Leila Dhanda, *Bonsai Culture*. New Delhi, 1984.
Paul Lesniewicz, *Bonsai. The Complete Guide to Art & Technique*. Dorset, 1984.
Peter Chan, *Bonsai. The Art of Growing and Keeping Miniature Trees*. London, 1993.

Bonsais on front and back cover and pages 10, 12, 17, 20-21, 25, 26, 28 (below), 33, 35, 43, 62 belong to Dr Leila Dhanda.
Bonsais on pages 3, 13, 16, 31 belong to Dr Hussain Tayebhoy.
Bonsais on pages 14-15, 19, 22, 23, 27, 28 (above), 29, 30, 34, 49, 54-58 belong to Ms Kiran Misra.

Charts on pages 35 and 63 are reproduced from Peter Chan, *Bonsai. The Art of Growing and Keeping Miniature Trees.*

CONTENTS

Introduction

In Japanese, bonsai (pronounced 'bone'-sai) means a plant or a tree grown in a pot. 'Bon' is a tray and 'sai' is a tree or plant. It is a misconception that bonsais are created by savagery or starvation. In reality bonsais are created through routine gardening and horticultural techniques such as pruning and potting. The technique of bonsai originated in China but it was the Japanese who really transformed it into an art. The Japanese, being innovative, made bonsais not only out of trees but out of shrubs and creepers too. From the Orient the art of bonsai travelled West and took root everywhere as a living and growing art form. The bonsai grower should realise that in trying to create an illusion of a mature tree in dwarf form, the soil, plant and pot must blend with each other to create a living object of beauty to be enjoyed by everyone.

Since bonsais are small they are commonly mistaken for indoor plants. Actually they should remain in conditions that are natural to their growth. Age is not a prerequisite of quality. Therefore, to be able to train a shrub, creeper or a young sapling into a tree and to make it grow in a small container we must know the features of a tree.

The trunk of a tree is broader at the base and tapers at the top. The crown of the tree is either round or conical depending upon the species. A third of the trunk from its base is normally free of branches. On the next one-third of the trunk grow the main branches. The branches fan outwards and bend downwards. Branches on the top third of the trunk are less spread out than the lower branches. In fact the entire branch system forms a triangle.

The root system of a tree consists of a very long tap root which helps to anchor the tree into the soil. The fibrous roots grow from this main root and absorb minerals and water from the soil. Once the features and functions of various parts of a tree are clear you will be able to train the tree with the help of pruning and potting into a bonsai. Your bonsai

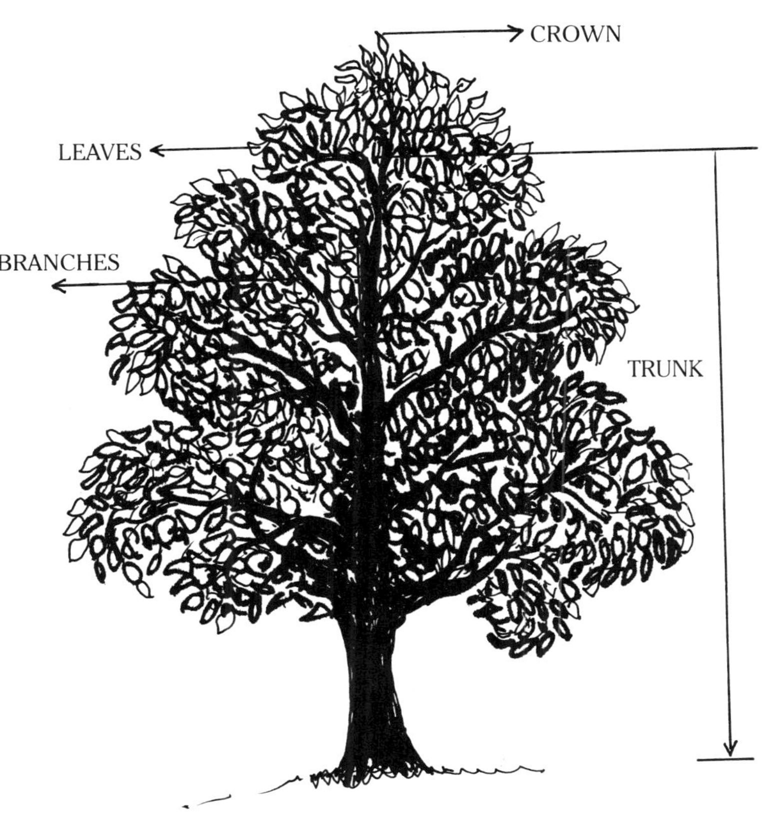

must respect the discipline imposed by the Japanese masters but need not be limited by the hard and fast rules laid down by them. Let your own aesthetic sense guide you.

Starting Out

Bonsais can be created by various methods, each with its own advantages and disadvantages.

Seeds

You can grow a bonsai from a seed. This is a very slow process. First, let the seed develop into a seedling, then a young sapling, which can then be pruned and shaped to create a bonsai.

Cuttings

Those who are too impatient to start from scratch with a seed can start from cuttings. Generally, cuttings of suitable plants are taken from their stems at the right season, and with the help of a rooting hormone planted till they take root. Then as they grow they are trained into a bonsai. This is a far quicker method.

Plant showing (i) aerial and (ii) ground layering.

Layering

The method of layering is suitable for shrubs and woody climbers. In every plant the sap runs up the trunk and branches. If this sap is intercepted it is capable of producing new roots: later the branch can be separated and grown as an individual plant. Sometimes a branch if grown separately may make a good bonsai. Separate it by doing aerial or ground layering. The best time for layering is the growing season, as for example the monsoon in India.

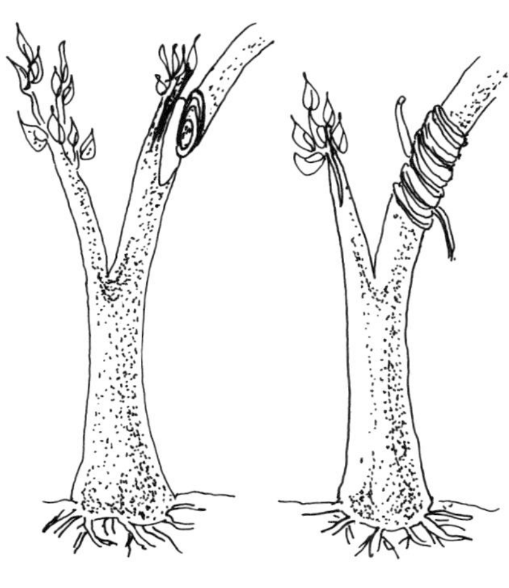

Grafting

Grafting is suitable for flowering and fruiting trees. The disadvantage is that it leaves an ugly mark which can, of course, be hidden by arranging the branches carefully.

An example of grafting

Nursery Plants

For a beginner, starting a bonsai from a nursery plant is probably the best method. Select a healthy plant which has a thick trunk and a number of branches. From such a plant, within a short time and with careful pruning and wiring, you will be able to create your future bonsai.

Plants from the Countryside

This includes looking for small trees which are found in very exposed situations, like in the countryside. Trees with stunted growth, or trees struggling to grow between rocks and in poor soil are the best choice. These should be carefully dug out, shaped and immediately planted as bonsai. If the roots are not sufficient you can plant the tree in the ground, dig it out a year later and pot it as a bonsai.

How to Choose Your Plant

The main points to be taken into account while choosing a plant for your bonsai are that it should be a hardy plant and the size of the leaves (or needles in case of conifers) should be small and compact. Its flowers and fruits should be small otherwise they will look disproportionate on a small tree.

Conifers

In Japan, conifers provide a wide choice for making bonsais. We in India are not as fortunate. Among the conifers that grow in the Indian subcontinent or

Pinus roxburghii—19 years

in other regions with warmer winters, *Juniperus prostrata* and *Pinus roxburghii* are the ones most commonly used. The black pine does very well in colder climates. *Pinus roxburghii* is suitable for a large bonsai since the needles are very long and droop downwards. Those who live at higher altitudes can make bonsais out of *Cedrus deodara* (deodar), spruce (*Picea smithiana*), fir (*Abies pindru*) and cypress *(Cryptomeria japonica)*. *Podocarpus nerifolia* is a conifer which also does well in warmer areas.

Broad-leaved Trees

Broad-leaved or deciduous trees are mostly found in tropical and semi-tropical climates. Trees of the *Ficus* genus (the family Moraceae) are hardy and quick growing and within a few years grow

*Ficus retusa—
25-30 years*

into interesting bonsai. Some varieties of deciduous trees are: *Ficus benjamina, Ficus benjamina nuda, Ficus glomerata, Ficus benjamina comosa, Ficus retusa, Ficus virens, Ficus benghalensis, Ficus religiosa, Ficus panda* and *Ficus longisland.* Some variegated species have also been developed. Some trees, like the

Ficus benjamina— 8 years

Ficus retusa— 6 years

Ficus virens produce aerial as well as thick spreading roots on the surface which add an illusion of age to the bonsai. *Ficus benghalensis* also produces aerial roots. *Tamarindus indica* (tamarind) of the sub-

Diospyrus montana—
5 years

Honeysuckle—
8 years

family Caesalpiniaceae is among the most beautiful trees that can be trained into a bonsai. In the same family is *Haematoxylon campechianum* which can be trained well. *Prosopis juliflora* and *Pithecellobium dulce* are hardy, drought resistant trees which can be trained as good bonsais. *Diospyros montana* of the family Ebenaceae is also good for making into a bonsai. From the elm family the *Celtis australis* and *Holoptelea integrifolia* both make beautiful bonsais but are difficult to obtain as they are wild trees. *Gingko biloba*, the maidenhair tree, prefers a cooler climate. *Casuarina equisetifolia* of the Casuarinaceae family grows well as a bonsai, as also the *Cinnamomum camphora*. Among the deciduous trees that do well as bonsais at higher altitudes and in cooler climates are the maple, sycamore and hornbeam.

Flowering and Fruiting Trees

The flowers and fruits of a tree do not reduce in size once it has been trained into a bonsai. Therefore it is preferable to choose plants or trees which will bear small sized flowers and fruits so that they are

Hibiscus—18 years

Pomegranate—8 years

in proportion to the size of the bonsai. For example, a grapefruit would look ungainly hanging from the branches of a bonsai tree. Many varieties of *Prunus persica* (peach) and numerous species of *Prunus domestica* (plum) are very suitable. Pear and almond trees can also be selected. Crab apple is suited to the cooler climate of the hills. Many varieties of cherry as well as apricot also do well. Hawthorn also makes a good bonsai. Mulberry (morus of the Moraceae family) grows very well in most parts of the Indian subcontinent. The wild variety of mulberry does better because of its smaller leaves. The *Ficus carica* (fig) has very interesting fruits. The bottlebrush (*Callistemon lanceolatus*) of the Myrtaceae family makes a very majestic bonsai. Its branches droop downwards and flowers appear at their tips. The dwarf guava, *Psidium cattleianum,* is also suitable for a bonsai because of its pretty flowers and fruits. Some of the acacias belonging to the sub-family Mimosaceae may also be tried, especially the *Acacia farnesiana.* The small variety of bauhinia and the *Averrhoa carambola* of the Oxalidaceae family develop into good bonsais. The *Mimusops elengi* of the Sapotaceae family is easy to train, as also the *Jacaranda mimosifolia.* The wood-apple or *Feronia limonia* of the Rutaceae family is another interesting plant for bonsai.

Shrubs

Shrubs which have been found suitable for making bonsais are the *Malpighia coccigera* of the Malpighiaceae family, the *Citrus japonica* (Chinese orange) of the Rutaceae family as well as the *Triphasia trifolia* and *Murraya exotica* of the same family. The calliandra species are also very popular, specially *Calliandra brevipes.* In the same family are popular bauhinias. From the rose family we have the flowering quince which is very interesting. *Cotoneaster microphylla* may also be trained in colder climates to obtain a very small bonsai. Varieties of azaleas also do well in cooler climates. The dwarf variety of the *Gardenia fortunei* with small leaves and flowers is very suitable. *Punica granatum* or 'nana', a pomegranate of the Punicaceae family is a dwarf shrub which bears interesting flowers and fruits. The *Carissa spinarum* of the Apocynaceae family is very hardy. Others shrubs are *Euphorbia splendens,* commonly known as kiss-me-quick of the Euphorbeaceae family. The *Nyctanthes arbor-tristis* of the Oleaceae family can also be tried. *Duranta repens* of the Verbenaceae family, particularly the variegated one, takes on a good shape with constant training.

Boungainvillaea Shobra —4 years

Creepers

The bougainvillaea of the Nyctaginaceae family is an interesting and hardy creeper which needs very little care. Bougainvillaeas must be trained very carefully, as the branches may snap while wiring. They should be potted only when they have developed good roots. Indian varieties which do well are:

Lady Mary Baring	Yellow
Shobra	White
Cherry Blossom	Pink and white
Mahara	Magenta purple
Sanderiana	Light purple
Roseville's Delight	Orange
Begum Sikandar	Light pink round edges, delicate colour, rest white
Blondie	Orange red changing to light pink
Bois-de-Rose	Slow growing, biscuit colour
Krumbiegal	Reddish purple
Lilacina	Mauve
Cyperi	Light mauve, restricted growth
Los Banos Beauty	Dusty pink—double bracted
Mrs Butt	Red purple
Rao	Variegated leaves—red bracts—young shoots and pinkish leaves
Refulgens	Purplish—small flowers
Tomato Red	Dark colour
Dr H. B. Singh	Light mauve
Zakiriana	Pinkish
Mrs H. C. Buck	Rosy purple

Bougainvillaea Cherry Blossom —18 years

Bougainvillaea Glabra —6 years

Other creepers you can consider are the red *Clerodendron splendens* of the Verbenaceae family or the star jasmine *(Trachelospermum jasminoides)* of the Apocynaceae family. A creeper with beautiful yellow flowers is the *Banisteria laurifolia* of the Malpighiaceae family. Another variety is the *Petrea volubilis* of the Verbenaceae family, with violet and

Bougainvillaea— 7 years

mauve flowers, or the honeysuckle *(Lonicera japonica)* of the Caprifoliaceae family. This last trains very well as a cascade and can also be grown over a rock. The *Wisteria sinensis* with its beautiful purple or white flowers is suitable for cooler places.

Foliage Plants

Certain plants may be chosen for their foliage. A bamboo, especially the dwarf variety, can be made

Bamboo Grove— 3 years

into a grove. The *Nandina domestica* of the Berberidaceae family has a very delicate appearance. The *Crassula argentea* (jade), a succulent of the Crassulaceae family, is very popular and is easily shaped to look like a tree.

Styles

The art of the bonsai lies in imitating nature as best as you can. Keeping this in mind, observe the way trees grow around you, and the shapes they acquire. Bonsais are trained into various styles. You do not have to strictly adhere to the rules of a particular style, but knowledge of the basic principles governing these rules is helpful if you wish to develop a natural-looking bonsai. The various styles are: *formal upright, informal upright, slanting, windswept, semi-cascade, cascade, broom,* bunjin *or literati, multiple trunks, group planting, rock planting, raft style and mame bonsais.* The Japanese have many more styles but those mentioned above are the basic ones.

Formal Upright Style

In this style the tree grows in an upright manner. It has a straight tapering trunk with thick roots fanning out and downwards into the soil. The first, lowest branch is kept at about one-third the height of the trunk to the left or right of the viewing side but never straight in front.

Juniperus chinensis—8 years

Proportions of Formal Upright Style

This first branch should be the most attractive, the longest and the thickest.

The second branch should be on the side a little above the first branch. If the second branch is on the opposite side it should be shorter but growing at an angle to the first. The third branch has to be at the back. This is the most important branch as it gives depth to the tree. These three branches grow horizontally outwards from the trunk, or slope slightly upwards or downwards depending on the species. The top third of the trunk is occupied by a network of the next three or four branches which are shorter, usually grow upwards and provide dense foliage to the upper part of the tree. The tree will end in a rounded or pointed top. Care should be taken that the branches have relatively equal access to sun and air. If the tree is planted in a round or square pot it should be planted in the centre. If it is planted in an oval or rectangular pot then the pot should be divided into three equal parts and the tree planted in the junction between two of these divisions. The longer of the two front branches will look best spread over two-thirds of the pot and the opposite branch over its smaller remaining side.

Informal Upright Style

Here the tree grows upwards as in the formal upright style but the trunk has well balanced curves and the top of the tree should be slightly tilting towards the viewing side. The other rules regarding root and branch

*Holoptelea integrifolia—
22 years*

arrangement and position in the container are the same as those for the formal upright style.

Slanting Style

In this style the tree grows at a slant of about 45° to the left or right. The lower branches spread out in the direction opposite to the slant of the tree. The branches are shorter on the acute inner angle and longer on the outer. The top is bent slightly forward and the tree is planted usually to one

Araucaria excelsa—
29 years
(slanting style)

side of an oval or rectangular pot so that a large part of it is above part of the container. The main branches are arranged as in the formal upright style.

Windswept Style

Here one side of the tree is free of branches. The whole tree should give the impression of having been blown in one direction by strong winds.

Malpighia coccigera—10 years (windswept style)

Semi-Cascade and Full Cascade

Here, as the name implies, the tree falls partially or fully over the pot to one side. In the semi-cascade style the trunk grows upwards for some length then bends downwards but never

Bougainvillaea—Shobra
4 years (semi-cascade style)

Juniperus—
10 years (full cascade style)

below the base of the pot. In the cascade style the tree grows a little upwards and then falls steeply below the base of the pot. In both cases the main branches can be identified. A full cascade has to be potted in a tall pot. These styles imitate trees in nature that hang over cliffs and rocks.

Broom Style

This is an upright style with all the branches sprouting from the trunk growing in an upward direction to resemble an inverted broom.

Bunjin or Literati Style

Though artistic, this style is not governed by the rules of bonsai styling. The trunk is interesting with many curves and there are very few branches. Foliage is sparse and more than half the trunk is bare. There is no distinct arrangement of branches. With its powerful profile the bunjin style is characterised by a rugged miniaturism.

Juniperus prostrata—literati-jinned style

Twin or Multiple Trunks

In this style there are two trunks growing from the same root ball. Sometimes the two trees are placed close to each other to form the twin trunk. The trunks are so placed that one is slightly in front of the other. The branches of the two trunks are arranged as for a single trunk tree. Twin trunks can be trained as slanting, informal, windswept, and so on. Multiple trunks are

Longisland—
(twin trunk style)

a variant of twin trunks. The extra trunks provide the opportunity to grow a copse of bonsais. There can be differences in the height and thickness of the trunks. Try to ensure that you have an odd number of trunks. The group of trunks should have a front and back with spreading side and back branches coming from individual trunks from the right, and from a suitable angle.

Feronia limonia—
38 years
(multiple style)

Raft Style

This is an interesting variation that forms a forest. The branches from one side of the trunk are removed and the rest are all wired straight up. While planting, the trunk is laid horizontally with the root ball on one side of the container and the wired branches facing upward. Before it is laid in the soil the side of the trunk which has no branches is given notches, or a flap of bark is removed from under each wired branch, so that it will root. Rooting hormone can also be applied. The trunk is firmly fixed in the container. It is then covered with the soil, watered and looked after. After a period of time, the wired branches will take root.

Group Planting

Here the idea is to imitate nature and to plant several trees in a container in groups, resembling a forest. The Japanese favour planting an odd number of trees. The main tree should be at the front and a little off centre. The smaller trees go at the back.

Celtis australis—
13 years (group planting)

Rock Planting

Rocks and trees look marvellous together. Rock-grown bonsais are created in two ways:

In the hollow of a rock—A suitable plant is shaped. The tap root, if present, is partly removed and other roots are lightly clipped. The hollow of a rock is filled with soil. The plant is placed in the hollow, covered with more soil and finally with wet sphagnum moss. The entire soil and rock is covered and tied so that the soil does not wash away during watering. The plant is watered thoroughly with a fine hose. The sphagnum

moss lasts for nearly a year till the plant is well established.

On a rock with roots going into the container—A plant having long roots is shaped then the long roots are dipped into a thick solution of clay. The plant is placed over a rock which is placed in a container with some soil. The roots with sticky clay on them

Pomegranate—2 years. Plant growing over a rock

Shefflara arboricola—6 years
Roots going over the rock and into the container

are trained over the crevices of the rock and into the container. Then the root system is covered with more clay mixture. Finally, it is covered with moist soil. The whole rock is then covered with moist sphagnum moss and tied. The whole rock, tree and soil in the container is watered with a fine spray.

Mame

These are miniature bonsais measuring 5 to 15 cm (2-6 in) from the base of the trunk to the top of the tree. The training is the same as for other bonsais except that the rules are less rigidly followed. The choice of plant also has to be correct. Plants with very small leaves, flowers and fruit are more suitable. Mames need a lot of attention as they are grown in very little soil.

Mames—Ficus virens, Ficus religiosa, Carmona microphylla

Classifying Bonsais According to their Size

Given below are the standard sizes into which bonsais are classified:

Less than 5 cm (2 in)	Thimble or thumb-sized bonsai
5 to 15 cm (2-6 in)	Mame or miniature bonsai
15 to 30 cm (6-12 in)	Small bonsai
30 to 60 cm (12-24 in)	Medium-sized bonsai
60 to 120 cm (24-48 in)	Big bonsai
Over 120 cm (4 ft)	Very large bonsai

Soil, Containers, Accessories and Tools

To grow a healthy tree good soil is essential. Bonsais are no different. Each country has a different kind of soil so every bonsai grower uses a different soil mixture depending on its availability and suitability.

Clockwise from left: *Garden soil; organic manure; leaf mould; coarse sand; a mixture of the above in varying proportions*

Soil

A good soil mixture should be able to supply the plant's needs for minerals and oxygen for at least a year. The texture should allow drainage of excess water to avoid waterlogging and rotting of fine roots, yet be able to retain enough moisture to enable the plant access to a constant supply of water. Thus a good compost should contain loam, humus and coarse sand in varying proportions according to the need of the plant. It should be free from disease, stones or lumps. The Japanese sieve their soil through meshes of different sizes and get soils of different grades which they then use. One way of making compost is to take equal parts of garden soil and organic manure, mix well, then to eight parts of this mixture add one part of coarse sand. You can also add various supplements, like bone meal, if you think the plant needs it. This is then mixed well and used. As conifers need better drainage you can add more leaf mould and sand to the soil for these trees. This means a changed ratio of one part sand to six parts loam mixture.

Containers

The choice of container depends on the style of your

Containers of various shapes and sizes

bonsai. A good container should be stable, well finished, with a good drainage hole. The container should blend well with the plant and add to its beauty. It can be made of a variety of materials. Ceramic pots glazed from the outside and unglazed from the inside are very popular. Terracotta pots (clay) are also used. They are available in different shapes, sizes and depths. Common shapes are rectangular, oval, square and round. Tall pots are used for cascade styles and trays for group planting. Bonsais can also be trained on slates and flat stones. Pots with feet

Decorative stands and bases for display of bonsai pots

are better because they protect the plant from insects creeping in through the drainage hole. Pots are available in all colours but natural earthy colours are better than bright colours. Decorative pots are not recommended as they tend to overshadow the plant.

Accessories

Stones can be used to enhance the beauty of your bonsai. Moss growing on old walls and damp places can be scraped off and placed on top of the soil for aesthetic reasons. It also helps to keep the soil from being washed away during watering and keeps the plant cool during the hot summers.

Tools

The basic tools needed are:

- Simple garden tools;
- Pruning clippers;
- Long handled slender shears;
- Wire cutter;
- Wire mesh / Plastic mesh;
- Potting sticks—one foot long pointed sticks which look like chopsticks, or number 8 knitting needles;
- Concave branch cutter;

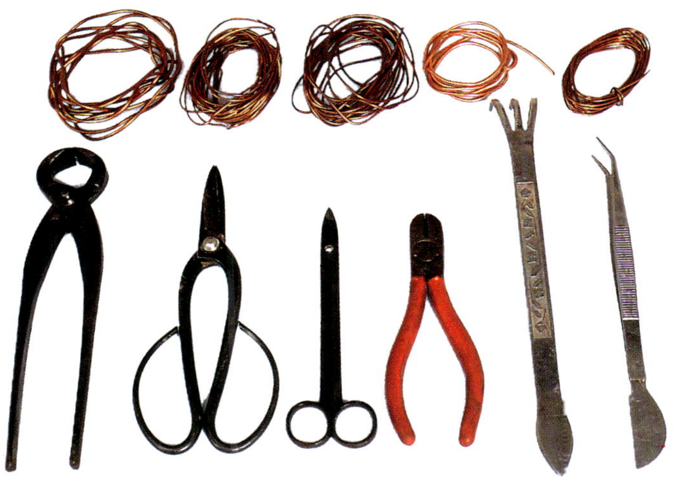

- Copper wire of various grades (no.14, 16, 19, 23) or aluminium wire of various grades (anodized aluminium wire is more pliable, inert and cheaper).

Care of Tools: All tools should be cleaned after use and then wiped with an oily rag to keep rust at bay.

Getting Ahead

Now that you have your plant, your container, the tools and the correct soil you can think about potting. To start training and potting a bonsai the correct season should be taken into consideration. The best time is when the sap is rising and leaf buds are developing. In India, in some species the sap rises between mid-December and early April. Another good potting season in India is during the monsoon, which is equivalent to spring in other countries.

Step I—*Choosing Your Plant*: The first thing to do when you get a plant to be trained as a bonsai is to study it at eye level from all sides taking decisions about its style, front, back, and finished height. A view of the entire trunk of the tree can be had by looking at it from the front. The bonsai should always lean slightly forward to give the best view of the tree. The shape, size and colour of the pot for the future mature bonsai is also decided.

Remove all the dead branches and all lower branches from the main trunk till one-third of the trunk is bare. The three primary branches to be retained are chosen. They

Step1 (a)—Plant from a nursery to be trained into a bonsai.

Step1 (b)—Removing of redundant branches

are shortened if wiring is not required, or shortened later after wiring. The cut is always made at a slant just above a growing bud. If branches are growing opposite each other, one of them is removed. If there is a branch growing just above the other, one of them is removed so that the plant is mostly left with alternate branches. Sometimes a branch may be left at the base of the trunk for a while until the trunk thickens. Then, later, it is removed. The desired height of the tree has to be decided so that the plant can be clipped at a certain height. Sometimes

Step1 (c)—Plant with only the required branches and height, ready for wiring and potting.

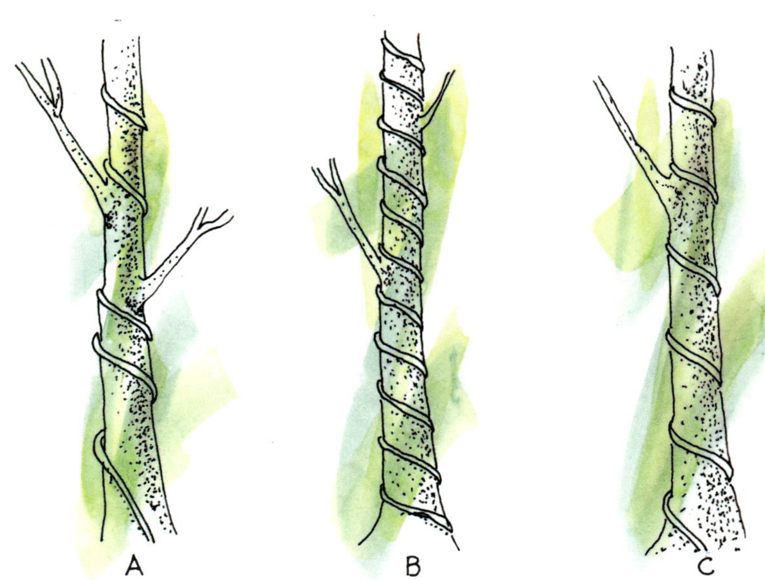

Wiring of Trunk
A. Incorrect wiring of trunk. B. Incorrect spacing. C. Correctly spaced wiring.

Correct way of bending a branch after wiring.

A plant after wiring.

one small top branch can be wired to give the plant a new crown. All excessive foliage is removed from the plant so that the entire branch pattern and the trunk is visible. All the finer branches are pruned back a little. Now, if a certain branch or the trunk has to be given a particular shape, train it as you wish with the help of anodized copper wire. Aluminium wires may also be used.

Step 2—*Shaping and Wiring:* Copper or aluminium wire and a wire cutter is all the equipment required for wiring. Sometimes a clamp or trunk wrench enables you to bend the trunk or larger branches to the required shape. The technique consists of wrapping metal wire of the right gauge (depending on the thickness of the branch or trunk) around the trunk, working upwards from the lower end. To wire the trunk, cut sufficient length of wire to go around the trunk of the tree chosen. Push one end firmly into the soil close to the back of the base of the tree. Securing the lower end with one hand turn the wire spirally around the trunk till the end of the trunk is reached. Each spiral is held in position with one hand before another spiral is made. In this way the correct degree of tension is maintained.

Juniperus prostrata—
5 years (wired shaping)

The wire should not be so tight as to interfere with the circulation but should be tight enough to hold the bends in place. The distance between the spirals should be equal, neither too close nor too far apart. Working carefully with both hands, the trunk can now be bent into position.

If the branches are to be shaped, they are wired in the same way. One end of the wire is anchored over the fork where the branch grows from the trunk. One turn is taken around the trunk to hold the wire in position then the spirals are wound around the branch in a clockwise direction for right hand branches and anti-clockwise for the left hand branches. The tips of the wires are bent back to finish off. Then the branch is bent into the desired position. Sometimes when two branches are close together they can be wired with just one length of wire by commencing from the centre of the wire. Holding the wire at the centre, first one branch is wired then the other. All wires must be left in place for a period of 3-6 months after which they should be removed. Ensure by regular checking that the wire does not cut into the bark and leave ugly scars.

Among the other methods of training a plant are bending a branch down by using a stone weight, or tying the branch and trunk together with a wire. A

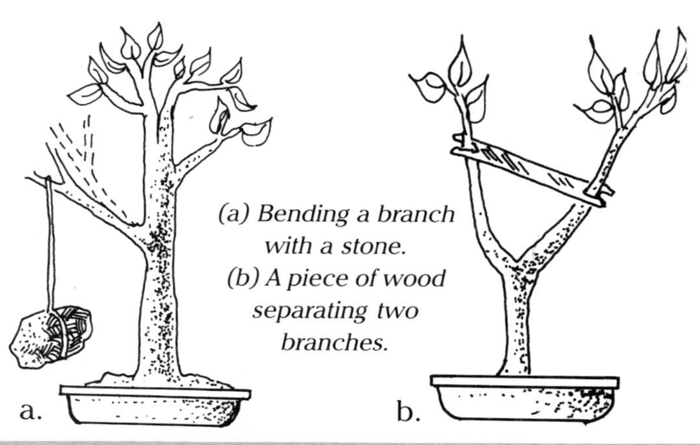

(a) Bending a branch with a stone.
(b) A piece of wood separating two branches.

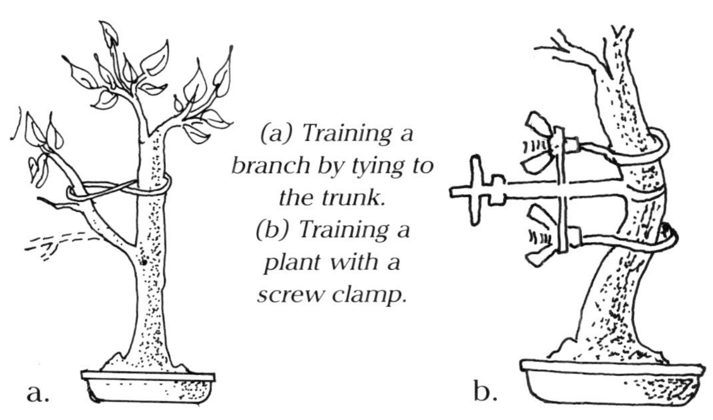

(a) Training a branch by tying to the trunk.
(b) Training a plant with a screw clamp.

piece of wood can also be used to hold two branches apart, or a screw clamp can be used to give a curve to a trunk.

Step 3—*Potting:* After the plant is shaped and wired the chosen pot is prepared (as shown on pages 56-57, steps 7-10). The pot must be dry and clean. The drainage holes are covered with pieces of plastic mesh or crocks (broken pieces of a pot). Over the bottom of the pot, spread a layer of coarse soil. Follow this with a layer of main soil. The soil should be moist, neither too dry nor too wet. The plant is removed from its pot by holding its base and inverting the pot. The earth is gently shaken off or removed with a pointed stick until half or one-third of the original soil is left. If there are any earthworms they should be removed. Now is the time for root pruning. This will depend upon the amount of foliage on the plant. If the roots are scanty then the foliage has to be proportionately reduced so that the scanty roots can support the plant. Look for the tap root (the long main root). If there are plenty of fine roots remove the tap root completely. Otherwise, remove just one-third of the tap root. Over a period of two or three years plenty of fine roots will have grown and the tap

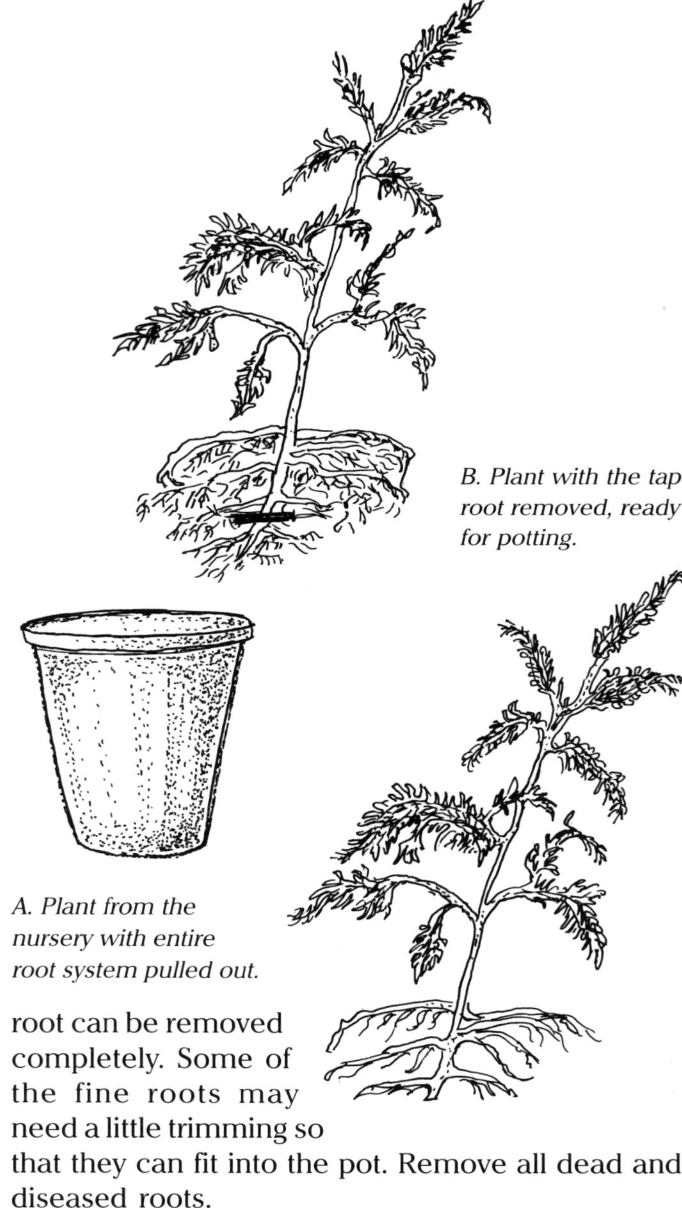

B. Plant with the tap root removed, ready for potting.

A. Plant from the nursery with entire root system pulled out.

root can be removed completely. Some of the fine roots may need a little trimming so that they can fit into the pot. Remove all dead and diseased roots.

The plant with its pruned roots is now placed in position over the soil in the pot. If the root ball is very thick it is held in position by tying it with a piece of wire which is passed through the drainage holes.

The large surface roots are spread out and more soil put into the pot till the plant is held firmly in position. With the help of a chopstick or a pointed potting stick push the soil well into the roots so that no air pockets are left (see Step 11 of section on repotting). If a growing root comes across an air pocket it will have nowhere to go and eventually die, thus harming the plant. The top of the container

The finished plant in its bonsai pot.

can be spread with a very fine layer of top soil which is gently pressed down by hand or with a small trowel. Now, if you want, pieces of green moss can be pressed on top of the soil, except on the surface roots if you want to leave them uncovered. Exposed surface roots lend an appearance of age to the bonsai. Sometimes when drastic root pruning is

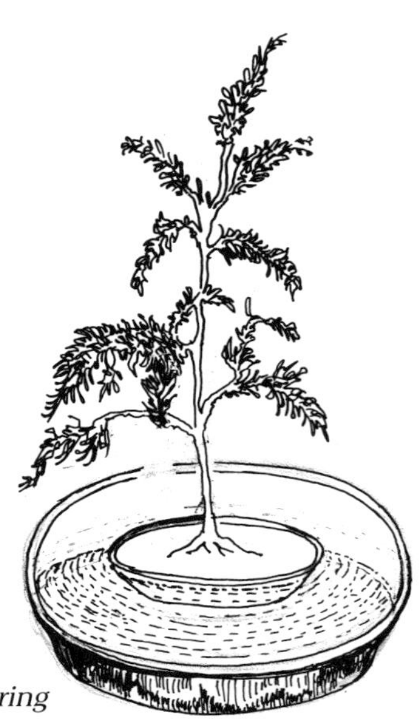
Step 4—Watering

done soil may be built up around the trunk to form a mound of earth.

Step 4—*Watering:* The first watering is the most important. This is done by standing the pot in a basin filled with water to just below the top of the bonsai pot. The water gets absorbed from the drainage holes via capillary action. In a short time the top will be wet and the plant thoroughly watered. Now keep the bonsai in a place sheltered from the sun and wind for a few days before gradually exposing it to the elements. The second watering should be done when the top soil starts showing signs of drying. This is done with a normal watering can.

Bonsais need plenty of water and food to be able to thrive. Since their roots cannot spread in search of water and food they are totally dependent on you. The best time to water is early morning or evening. Watering is done whenever the top soil starts drying. Shower the foliage thoroughly to wash away any dust and keep your bonsai looking fresh. In the summer water bonsais twice a day. Dormant plants and conifers need less water.

Pruning and Trimming

The purpose of pruning is to give the plant a particular shape and to control its growth by trimming the branches and leaves. The equipment required for pruning are a pair of good scissors for trimming the smaller branches and leaves and a concave cutter for the bigger branches.

Pruning of Ficus

Pruning

The first pruning is drastic. It is done at the time of original potting to achieve a certain shape. All branches which are either directly opposite each other, or redundant are removed. The plant is normally left with alternate branches. Pruning at a later stage is done to keep the tree in shape. Excessively long branches should be shortened.

If you look carefully, the branch which has to be cut back will have new buds growing on it in various directions. When cutting back a branch make sure to cut it near a growing bud, checking the direction

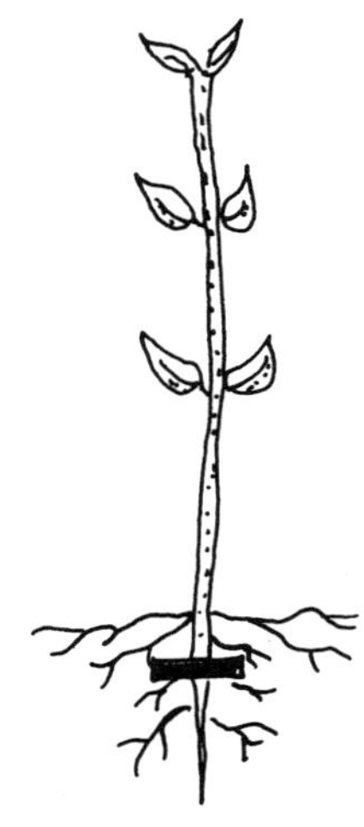

The central tap root of this young seedling destined to become a bonsai should be gradually removed.

Plant should be cut just above a growing bud. The new shoot will grow in the direction the bud is facing.

in which the bud is pointing (and always leaving a pair of leaves on the branch). This is important because the new growth will be in that direction. Cuts should be clean so that the tree can heal quickly. Coniferous trees, particularly pines, have to be pruned very carefully because they will not bud from old wood. Repeated pruning in deciduous trees will produce smaller leaves, and in conifers smaller needles.

Pinching of Pine (a)

Pinching of Pine (b)

Pinching of Juniper (a)

Pinching of Juniper (b)

Leaf Pruning

This is mostly done on healthy deciduous trees. The leaves are cut off from each branch leaving a portion of stem intact so that the neighbouring bud is not harmed by mistake. After a fortnight new leaves will appear. In this way you are forcing the plant to have another crop of leaves in the same season. This is done mainly to reduce the size of the leaves. Sometimes all the leaves of the plant are cut along the midrib.

Trimming or Pinching

Trimming or pinching (illustrated on previous page) is done throughout the life of a bonsai to maintain the quality of the tree's foliage. Pinching back helps preserve the shape of the plant, by inhibiting the natural exuberance of the growth. Gradually the

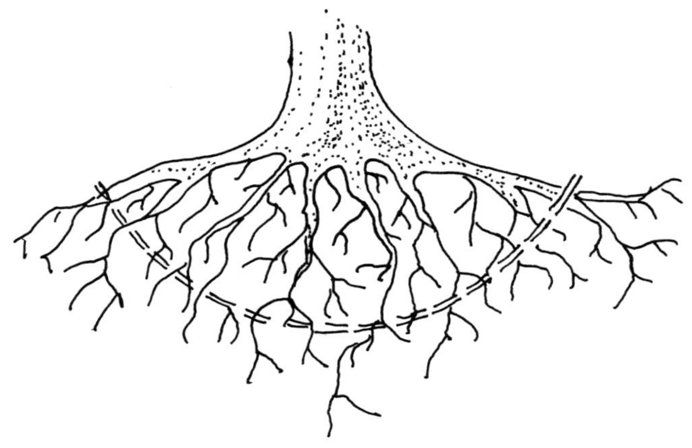

Fibrous roots being trimmed.

smaller branches become finer forming an interesting network. The leaves also become smaller. The number of times the tree has to be trimmed varies depending on the growth of the tree. Trimming should be stopped before flowering. When new growth appears all branches are pruned back to two or three leaves. During the growing season, plants need a lot of trimming. In conifers like juniper and pine you have to constantly pinch back the new growth. Do not use scissors for trimming conifers as they tend to damage the remaining needles as well as the buds.

Feeding Your Bonsai

Bonsais are dwarfed not by starving them of food but by the technique of pruning foliage and roots. In order to keep them healthy we have to feed them regularly with natural or artificial fertilisers. Organic manures are freely available. There are also very good artificial fertilisers containing a correct proportion of nitrogen, potassium and phosphorus needed by plants. Artificial fertilisers should be applied in a very weak solution. It is always better to underfeed than overfeed.

Here is a recipe for a very useful fertiliser. Place 1 kg of any oil cake in a bucket that can hold 10 litres. Add water up to 2 inches of the rim so that the manure does not overflow after fermenting. Add 25 gms of wood ash (this helps reduce the acidity of the soil). Stir the mixture, cover it and let it ferment for 2 to 3 weeks. Dilute this solution 15 times and use it for your bonsais once a week.

Another way is to mix the oil cake with a little water and let it ferment for two to three weeks. Then knead it, make small flat balls and dry in the sun. You can use one or two balls on each bonsai for slow manuring. Superphosphate is very good for fruiting and flowering plants. A regular schedule should be followed for manuring. Your bonsai should be manured once a week or once a fortnight. Pines need less manure. No manuring is done during the dormant period. After potting or repotting, do not use manure for at least a month or till the roots are well established. Fertilisers should not be used on weak or diseased plants.

Repotting

Since bonsais are pot-bound plants they have to be repotted regularly to prune the overgrown roots, remove the nutrient-depleted soil and replenish the compost (as illustrated stepwise below). In places where the climate is tropical or

Step 1—Plant to be repotted *Step 2—Plant after pruning*

sub-tropical plants grow very rapidly, therefore bonsais have to be repotted every year or once in two years. Slow growing trees can be left undisturbed for two to three years. The right time for repotting is just when new buds start appearing.

Step 3—Plant removed from bonsai pot

Step 4—Roots being teased

In India, this happens during spring or in the monsoons. Before repotting, the

Step 5—Excess roots being removed

Step 6—Plants with roots removed

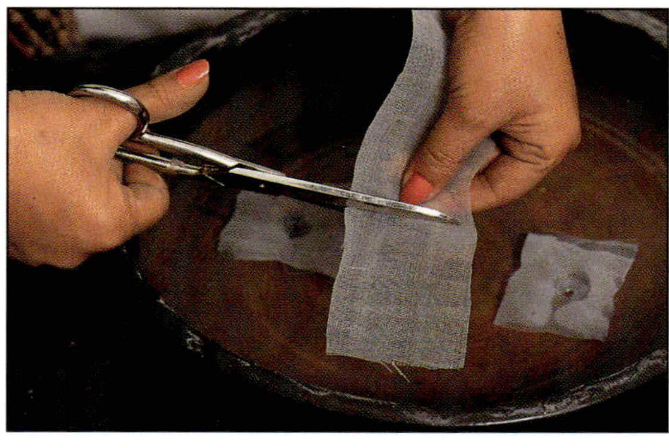

Step 7—Covering the drain holes with a wire mesh

same process of pruning and re-wiring is repeated where necessary. About 70 per cent of the old soil is removed, the root ball is teased and excess fibrous roots are trimmed. If there are any thick roots these

Step 8—Pot with covered drain holes

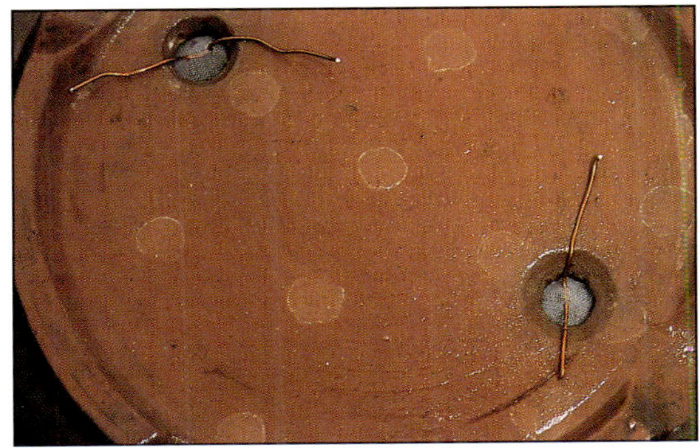

Step 9—Back of the pot

Step 10—Putting the prepared soil into the pot

are removed. Trimming of roots will induce further root development. The pot is cleaned and prepared in the same manner as for potting. The

Step 11—Placing the plant in the pot and pushing the soil in with chopsticks

Step 12—First watering

Step 13—Finished plant

bonsai is replanted, and the pot is filled with fresh compost, covered once more with moss and watered. The pot is kept in a sheltered place for some time till the plant recovers and then it is kept out in the open and watered normally.

Other Routine Measures

The drainage hole of the pot should be checked regularly for blockage. Weeds should be removed. The bonsai should be kept clean and all the dead leaves and flowers removed. If the top soil is washed away it should be replaced. Plants which receive sunlight only on one side should be turned regularly. Plants should be checked for diseases and dealt with accordingly. Scales can be removed from leaves and branches by sponging them with methylated spirit.

Pests and Diseases

Bonsais, like any other plants, are susceptible to attacks from pests and diseases. You have to be very alert when looking for disease symptoms in your bonsai because it is very painful to lose even a single branch as it mars the beauty of the plant. Whenever a bonsai looks unhealthy and diseased it must be attended to immediately. Prevention is better than cure. This is the key to success in protecting your bonsai against diseases. For most fungal diseases spray with a suitable fungicide. Plants affected by virus normally have no cure. Generally, the affected area has to be removed and destroyed, but to check the attack of any virus one should check the carrier and for that a general insecticide in mild solution can be sprayed. Any insect or larvae seen on the plant should be removed as they destroy the leaves and suck the cell sap. Following a regular, balanced nutritional schedule for your plant prevents any deficiency and increases its immunity to any parasitic diseases.

Displaying Your Bonsai

Bonsais displayed inside the house should be at eye level. They can be placed on suitable stands and look best against plain backgrounds. They should be kept indoors just for a day or two. For exhibiting purposes the plant must be correctly named, the container along with the plant properly cleaned and the plant neatly pruned well in advance of the show. All leaves should be wiped clean.

Record Keeping

It is a good idea to keep a detailed record of each bonsai. The date when the bonsai was started, the manner in which it was started (whether from a seed, a nursery plant or by grafting) are all facts which are recorded. The date of periodical repotting and any change of container or style at the time of repotting should be noted. Thus a complete history of each plant can be maintained.

Location

All bonsais should be kept outdoors where they receive at least three to four hours of sunshine and a free circulation of air. They should preferably be kept on stands or benches at an ideal height of three feet so that they can be viewed at eye level. They should not be kept on the ground as earthworms and other insects can crawl through the drainage holes. Moreover, the roots sometimes grow through the drainage holes and into the ground. If your bonsais are kept in a verandah they will receive sunlight from only one direction. Therefore they must be turned every two days so that all sides get sunlight and the plants do not grow in a lopsided manner. Plants need to be protected from strong winds as being small they may get blown away. They should also be protected from heavy rain as the soil will get washed away. In case the soil gets washed away it should be replaced immediately.

Age

The age of the bonsai is usually calculated from the time it is first planted in a bonsai container.

Aging Process

Here are a few tips to make your bonsai look mature:

1) To thicken the trunk keep the plant in the ground for two or more years. Keep pruning and wiring it to retain the shape. Dig up every year to trim the roots and replant in the ground.
2) You can train in a larger pot than necessary for two or more years.
3) Do not remove branches growing at the base because thickening takes place just below the branch. After thickening has taken place this branch can be removed.
4) Buy a plant with a thick trunk and shape it later.
5) During the growing season a wire is tied tightly round the trunk just below the soil. After thickening has taken place (usually after a season) remove the wire.
6) Encourage and bring to the surface the bare roots and spread them round the base of the trunk. In case surface roots are not well developed, remove a strip of bark all round the base of the trunk just above the roots and cover it with damp moss. Roots will develop all round the base. Remove extra roots and let a few of the remaining roots thicken.
7) Train three or more main branches to a horizontal position to give the tree a look of maturity.

8) An appearance of age can be given to the bonsai by giving certain branches a broken or dead look as though struck by lightning. In Japanese a dead tip of a trunk or branch is called *Jin*.

Juniperus prostrata—jinned branch.

Jinning: to make a *jin* one-third of the branch is broken or cut halfway from the back and pulled downwards in front. The bark is removed and the new hardwood exposed in a natural-looking tip. The tip must be rugged and pointed. It is then sand-papered and bleached with dilute citric acid. When it is dry it is painted with a lime sulphur mixture. To prepare this mixture, 55 gms of unslaked lime is mixed with half a litre of water and double this quantity of powdered sulphur is mixed with the same amount of water. The two mixtures are boiled together for about an hour. This mixture is applied twice a year to protect the dead wood. Parts of the trunk may also be peeled in the same way (to give the effect of age) and painted with lime sulphur mixture. In Japanese this is called *Shari*.

Bonsai Calendar

This book is for those living in the northern hemisphere. Corresponding seasons for the southern hemisphere are given in the chart below.

	Winter	Spring	Summer	Autumn
Northern hemisphere	Dec/Jan/Feb	Mar/Apr/May	Jun/Jul/Aug	Sept/Oct/Nov
Southern hemisphere	Jun/Jul/Aug	Sept/Oct/Nov	Dec/Jan/Feb	Mar/Apr/May

January: Normally this is a dormant period for most plants (in India pines are potted and repotted now). Do not give fertilisers in this period and protect plants from severe cold.

February: Season for repotting. All plants showing signs of growth can be potted and repotted. In the subcontinent peach and plum are potted and repotted in this month only.

March: Continue repotting. Plants showing vigorous growth should be pruned. In the subcontinent, this is the time for potting and repotting junipers.

April: Continue pruning. Discontinue all repotting.

May: Protect your plants from sun and hot winds in hot climates and start watering twice a day. Pruning continues. Feeding of plants is discontinued in hotter regions.

June: As in May. Prune plants showing vigorous growth.

July: With the onset of the monsoon this is the right time to pot and repot all plants (except conifers) in the subcontinent, especially bougeanvillaeas. In temperate zones commence watering as it is getting hot

August: In the subcontinent, continue as for July. In the temperate zones where the weather will be very warm now continue watering as often as necessary.

September: Potting and repotting stops for the subcontinent. Continue watering and feeding for all climate zones.

October: Reduce feeding because the growing season is coming to an end and all deciduous plants begin to shed their leaves.

November: Most deciduous trees start shedding leaves and become dormant so feeding should stop.

December: Protect plants from the severe cold. Time to pot and re-pot pines in India.

INDEX